Der Glaßmaler.

Einen Glaßmaler heist man mich/
In die Glässer kan schmeltzen ich/
Bildwerck/ manch herrliche Person/
Adelich Frauwen vnde Mann/
Sampt jren Kindern abgebild/
Vnd jres gschlechts Wappen vnd Schilt/
Daß man erkennen kan darbey/
Wann diß Geschlecht herkommen sey.

Der

An Introduction to
English Stained Glass

1
The head of the King Semei set amongst later fragments. The painted lines and
modelling are of great strength and simplicity. It comes from the south-east
transept clerestory of Canterbury Cathedral. Probably c.1180. Given by the
Rev. J. Wheatley. Ht. 36.2cms (C.854-1920)

An Introduction to

English Stained Glass

Michael Archer

Deputy Keeper, Department of Ceramics
Victoria & Albert Museum

Publishers, Inc. Owings Mills, Maryland

To Chloë and Joshua

Acknowledgements
I should like to thank all my colleagues in the Museum and those engaged
on the *Corpus Vitrearum* in England, Europe and America, who have helped
me in so many ways. I am particularly grateful to Claire Venner who typed
the manuscript and Christine Smith who took the admirable photographs.
Finally I should like to thank my children for their patience on many
expeditions looking at 'boring old stained glass' and above all my wife for
her enthusiastic participation in my research and writing.

Inquiries should be directed to
Stemmer House Publishers, Inc.
2627 Caves Road
Owings Mills, Maryland, 21117

First Edition

Library of Congress Cataloging in Publication Data

Archer, Michael.
    An introduction to English stained glass.

    (The V & A introductions to the decorative arts)
    Bibliography: p.
    1. Glass painting and staining–England–History. I. Title. II. Series:
Victoria & Albert Museum introductions to the decorative arts.
NK5343.A73 1986   748.592   85-20776
ISBN 0-88045-075-4

Of all the crafts practised in the middle ages the making of stained glass windows has probably changed the least. The earliest known manual is the *De diversis artibus* of Theophilus in which elaborate instructions are given on the techniques of painting, glass-making and metalworking. Theophilus seems likely to have been the pseudonym of a German Benedictine monk, Roger of Helmershausen, who probably wrote his treatise between 1110 and 1140. By this date the art of stained glass was well established and we know from other evidence (see page 9) that the necessary technical knowledge existed at least as early as the seventh century.

The use of lengths of lead to hold together pieces of glass appears to have evolved in the Byzantine world. This technique seems to have been unknown to the Romans who used cast or cylinder blown panes (see below) which were mounted in wooden frames. Such slabs were certainly used in England since examples have been found at Silchester and Chichester. In Italy, where the sunlight was strong, thin slabs of alabaster were sometimes used as in the Mausoleum of Galla Placidia in Ravenna (AD 440).

However glass or alabaster windows were both limited to the buildings of the wealthy, and at that time and for many centuries afterwards most windows were open apertures which could be closed by shutters. Sometimes they were filled with a translucent material mounted on a wooden frame. During the middle ages the normal arrangement was that the lower part of a window was open with a wooden shutter while the upper part was filled with a lattice of narrow flat battens to which were attached small pieces of horn or hide, parchment, linen or paper treated with oil or fat to give translucency. Windows of this sort were in use until the 18th century and even the secondary windows of important buildings were occasionally filled in this way.

Until the mid-16th century very little white and even less coloured glass was made in England and so glaziers depended on imports from the Rhineland area of the Duchy of Burgundy as well as from Normandy and Lorraine. The main patrons were monasteries, cathedrals and the richer parish churches and secular demand was limited to the King, the nobility and the wealthier merchants. Even clear glass windows were considered so valuable that they were moved in their wooden frames from one house to another and appear separately listed

2

in inventories. By the 1580s small tradesmen often had glass windows but glazing was not common in the houses of the very poor until the 19th century, despite an enormous growth in the supply of glass during the 17th and 18th centuries.

Little is known of the glass-making industry in England during the middle ages which was mainly limited to the Weald of Surrey and Sussex. In Roman times no coloured translucent window glass was made. Their white glass was produced with sand (silica) and burnt marine vegetation (soda). Similar raw materials were used in medieval northern Europe but with the substitution of beech-wood or bracken ash which provided potash rather than soda. Sand in its natural condition often contains iron-oxides which produce a green tinge, a characteristic of both Roman and medieval plain glass. This was not of course obtrusive in coloured glass which seems first to have been used for windows in the Byzantine world. The techniques of making coloured glass, known in its liquid state as 'metal', were comparatively simple and changed little. Metallic oxides were added to the pots or crucibles in which uncoloured glass had been melted. Cobalt supplied blue, while iron and copper in various forms produced red and green. Natural red pot-metal glass was too dark to transmit much light and so the medieval glass-maker evolved a technique of applying or 'flashing'

2
The making of glass by the 'muff' method as illustrated in Diderot's *Encyclopédie* of 1751-72

6

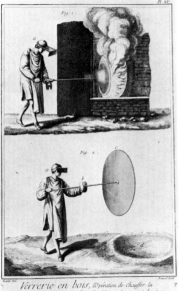

3

The blowing of 'crown' glass as illustrated in Diderot's *Encyclopédie* of 1751-72

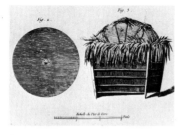

4

A disk of 'crown' glass showing the boss at the centre from which a 'bulls-eye' pane was cut, and a carrying crate packed out with straw

a thin layer of the coloured glass on to a sheet of clear white glass. A similar process was also used in the 15th century for the colour blue, when a lighter tone was required.

The conversion of molten glass into flat sheets was done by two quite distinct and rival methods known as cylinder-blown and crown. The former, sometimes called 'broad' or 'muff' glass was the method used in the Roman Empire and is the one mentioned by Theophilus. A bubble of molten glass was blown on the glass-blower's pipe or 'iron' into a cylindrical shape from which the extremities were cut off (plate 2). The cylinder that resulted was split lengthways with a hot iron and then reheated and opened out into a flat sheet which was finally put in a smaller 'annealing' oven to cool and harden. This method was widely used in Europe but particularly in the lower Rhineland and Hesse. It was also used in Bohemia and glass-makers from there came and set up in the Vosges mountains of Lorraine at the end of the 14th century. For over two hundred years this was the source of much of the coloured glass imported into England.

'Crown' glass was made by transferring the bubble of 'pot-metal' from the blowers' pipe to an iron rod or 'punty'. This rod was then spun or trundled between the worker's hands until by centrifugal action the opening where the pipe had been detached widened and the bubble spread itself into a large disk (plate 3). The point where the rod had been detached from the centre of the disk left a thick boss with a sharp scar in the middle, known as a 'bullion' or 'bull's-eye' (plate 4). When the disk had cooled it was cut into rectangular pieces. The crown method originated in the Islamic world and spread throughout Europe. It was used by a number of Norman glass-making families who supplied glass to England. In the early middle ages sheets of both muff and crown glass were small and thick, but by the end of the 14th century more ductile glass metal was available and much larger thinner and flatter pieces could be made.

With a stock of coloured glass the glazier could begin the process of making a window. He began by drawing a 'vidimus', a small sketch which could be modified until approved by the client. The design, once agreed, was drawn out full-size on a wooden table whitened with chalk or whitewash. Such a table was recently discovered at Girona in Spain, made up into a cupboard. It can be dated to the mid-14th century because it is painted with the lead lines of tracery lights which exactly correspond with windows of that date still extant in the Cathedral there. The lines drawn on the glaziers' table are often known as the 'cut-lines' since they define the shapes the varous pieces of coloured glass are to follow. They also show the lines of the proposed leading and the main details of the design such as human features, drapery, foliage, architecture and so forth. In the course of time paper took the place of the whitening on the table. The glazier indicated on the table the colours of the various pieces of glass and then cut these to shape. He did this with a notched tool known as a 'grozing

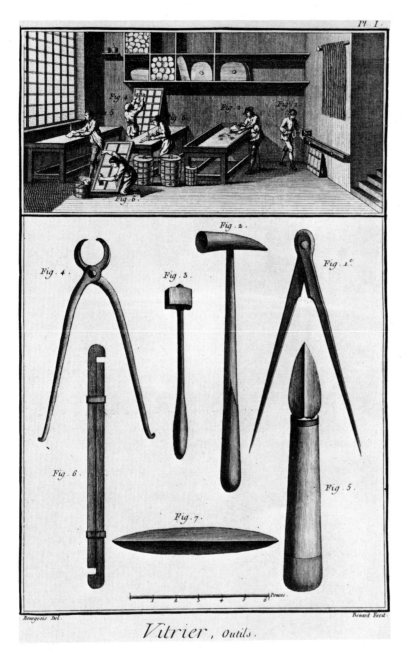

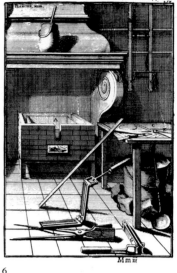

6

A cauldron for melting lead is shown with the ladle for filling the iron moulds (G) which lie on the floor in the foreground. An Illustration from André Félibien, *Des Principes de l'Architecture etc,* Paris, 1690

7

A lead mill showing, in the upper left, the H-shaped calm passing through the jaws of the mill. An illustration from André Félibien, *Des Principes de l'Architecture etc,* Paris, 1690

5

The glazier's tools including a grozing iron (6) and a view (above) of a workshop with men milling lead, cutting glass and making up plain glass windows. From Diderot's *Encyclopédie* of 1751-72

8

iron' (plate 5). This was a ponderous process made far easier in the 16th century with the introduction of the diamond cutter.

When all the pieces of coloured glass had been laid in their corresponding positions on the cartoon, he marked the underlying 'trace-lines' painted on the table on the upper surface of the glass. The pigment he used was a black enamel composed of iron or copper oxide mixed with a flux of powdered colourless glass. The design was then elaborated either by scratching through the black enamel or, from the 14th century onwards, by means of stippling to get more subtle effects of shading. The enamel pigment had then to be fused to the surface of the glass by being fired at a low temperature in a small kiln.

Once cut, painted and fired the pieces of glass were returned to the relevant parts of the design on the table. The retaining leads were then prepared and cut to the required lengths. Leads or 'calms' are of H section and were cast in wooden or iron moulds (plate 6). In the 16th century a lead mill was invented for their final shaping and leads treated in this way show ladder-like roulette marks on each side of the 'heart', as the central core is called, between the two flanges or 'crowns' which form the rebates that hold the glass in place (plate 7). When the pieces of glass had been placed in position, the retaining lengths of lead were bent to the right curves and laid round them. At this stage the glass had to be held firmly in place and this was done by driving long nails into the wood of the table; the leads were then soldered to each other with a hot iron. The glazier had previously decided on where to divide his window horizontally, generally at approximately 18 inch intervals, so that the panels which resulted would be of a convenient size and weight for transport. Finally he brushed a specially mixed cement into the leads so that wind and water could not penetrate.

When all the panels were completed, they were ready for insertion in the window. They were held in place in the masonry by means of iron supports known as 'saddle bars' to which they were tied with copper wires soldered on to the leads. This meant that each panel was suspended from above so that its weight did not need to be carried by the panel below. In windows which had comparatively narrow openings between the stone mullions, saddle bars alone provided sufficient support but in bigger windows vertical iron stanchions were introduced. In large windows of the 12th and 13th centuries, such as those at Canterbury, the iron bars follow the geometric lines, curved or straight, of the main divisions of the window design and play an important part in the general pattern. The same is true of the lead-lines which are at their most successful when they augment and accentuate the contours of the design.

The earliest documentary references to stained glass windows in England both relate to the archdiocese of York. Eddi in his life of St Wilfrid states that in about 670 the entry of birds and rain into the Saxon York Minster was prevented 'by means of glass, through which, however, the light shone within'. Bede tells how in 675 Benedict

8
Part of the ground of scrolling foliage
from one of the Trinity Chapel Ambulatory windows of Canterbury Cathedral. The semi-circular side would have
enclosed a roundel probably showing a
scene from the Life of Becket. c.1180–90.
Given by Mr John Hunt. Ht. 80.6cms
(C.2-1958)

9
A panel of *grisaille* glass painted with ivy
leaves. It is said to have come from York.
c.1300. Henry Vaughan Bequest.
Ht. 90.2cms (932-1900)

10

10
A shield of arms of the Percy family.
In the early Middle Ages coats of arms
were generally very simple. Early 14th
century. Ht. 20.3cms (C.203-1912)

11
A tracery light showing a donor and his
wife identified in the Latin inscription
as William Cele and his wife. Said to
have come from a church in Suffolk.
First half of the 14th century.
Ht. 52.4cms (C.202-1912)

11

Biscop imported workmen from Gaul to make windows for the monastery he founded at Monkwearmouth. We have some idea of how this
glass must have looked from the fragments excavated on the site of the
nearby monastery at Jarrow which flourished from 682 to about 870.
Some of these pieces are in carefully shaped forms which suggest
figurative subjects but the majority seem to have been part of a decorative mosaic of plain colours, sometimes with contrasting glass trails
fired on to the surface. Before the 12th century stained glass windows
must have been rare in northern Europe and it is not until about 1178,
when the first glazing programme at Canterbury Cathedral was under
way, that we find any considerable amount of English glass still surviving today.

The windows at Canterbury are of two basic types. The earliest
were originally in the high clerestory and consist of tall imposing
figures representing the forebears of Christ. They were painted on a
large scale and with simple, powerful lines which could easily be seen
from below (plate 1). Slightly later are the windows at a lower level in

the choir and presbytery aisles and the Trinity Chapel ambulatory. These windows are very large round-headed openings without mullions and are filled with small narrative panels of varying shapes set in a rich carpet of scrolling foliage (plate 8). They are supported by an elaborate armature of metal bars (ferramenta), many of which are carefully shaped to avoid cutting across the design. Like the clerestory figures these little scenes are painted with great dramatic power, and simple modelling using a kind of short-hand whereby a tree stands for a landscape and a roof with some columns represents a house or an interior. The predominant colours are dark, powerful reds and blues but with considerable areas of green, purple and yellow. All the subject matter was worked out with great care as part of an iconographic programme following a series of conventions.

These were already very sophisticated by the 12th century and continued to be used with further additions and modifications until the Reformation. An example are the so-called Types and Anti-Types, where one or two subjects from the Old Testament (Anti-Types) were chosen as being thought to foreshadow incidents in the New Testament (Types). Thus the Passage of the Red Sea was seen as prefiguring the Baptism of Christ. These complicated subjects were systematised in the *Biblia Pauperum* (the Bible of the Poor), which first appears in about 1300 and the *Speculum Humanae Salvationis* (the Mirror of Man's Salvation). Both continued in use throughout the middle ages, augmented by accounts of the lives and miracles of saints, both famous and obscure.

Canterbury was fortunate in possessing the remains of St Thomas à Becket who was credited with many miracles. He had been martyred in 1170 but a new shrine was made for his body in 1220 in the Trinity Chapel. In the early 13th century a number of miracle windows were installed and these continue and develop the style of the earlier narrative windows of the preceding century.

The only other considerable body of glass of this date in England is in Lincoln Cathedral. Here the major monument is the circular window in the north transept which contains a 'Day of Judgement' scene. Odd panels elsewhere in the Cathedral show that a large number of windows were glazed at this time.

It is clear however that in the second half of the 13th century a growing number of churches were installing painted windows and surviving fragments of these are to be found throughout the country. Few are of any great significance but it is worth noting those at Madley (Herefordshire), Westminster Abbey (the Jerusalem Chamber) and West Horsley (Surrey). This increased use of stained glass can be traced back to the influence of Abbot Suger. His new choir at St Denis of 1140-44 with its impressive glazing scheme was soon followed by the building and glazing of numerous cathedrals. The artists and craftsmen responsible were still mainly monks but this situation soon changed and increasingly laymen took over. Their workshops, however, continued to be based on large ecclesiastical foundations since these were the most important patrons both for new work and for repairs.

Although the builders of a church or cathedral would have wished to fill its windows with coloured glass as soon as possible, the money was not necessarily forthcoming immediately and the weather had to be kept out. Many windows were therefore glazed in clear glass and were often painted with patterns or foliage in black enamel. This economy coincided with a movement in the 12th century against luxurious decoration, notably in the Cistercian order, which exercised a restraining influence. The earliest window in England painted in this 'grisaille' is at Brabourne in Kent and dates from the late 12th century. It consists of a pattern of simple roundels and florets, while one at Stodmarsh in the same county is a little later and has roundels, quatrefoils and foliate scrolls. The largest and best known windows of this type are the so-called 'Five Sisters' in the north transept at York Minster (c. 1253). These are entirely painted with monochrome patterns of foliage and an occasional medallion of colour (plate 9). They are the only means by which we can form an impression of what a large area of 'grisaille' looked like. Such glass must have been common, particularly in cathedrals, as we learn, for example, from panels which have survived at Lincoln and Salisbury.

At Salisbury, too, are to be found some of the earliest shields of arms (c. 1270-80) to survive in England, those of the King and various noble families (plate 10). Generally such arms belong to the donors of windows and the understandable wish to be commemorated led not only to a proliferation of heraldic devices in stained glass as the Middle Ages advanced but also to actual representations of the donors themselves, depicted standing or kneeling in prayer. Such figures are found as early as the late 13th century and become common in the 14th (plate 11). A number of well preserved examples can be seen in the chapel at Merton College, Oxford where the donor, Henry de Mamesfield, appears twice in every window, flanking the figure of a saint in a single band of coloured glass. Above and below is 'grisaille' glass beautifully painted with branches of oak and set with a few small coloured roundels. The panes of 'grisaille' are shaped in most subtle patterns but such sophistication is unusual and a simple trellis of diamond-shaped 'quarries' became the norm.

Each of the figures is surmounted by an architectural canopy supported on shafts at the sides and topped with battlements and pinnacles to suggest a stone niche. Such a setting for figures or scenes soon became a conventional artistic solution and took up an increasingly large portion of the window as the 14th century progressed (plate 13). An illuminating comparison can be made between the so-called Pilgrimage window in the north aisle of York Minster and the west window close by. The former of about 1320-30 is very like the Merton glass, with small canopies over the figure subjects which are

12
The Annunciation to the Shepherds. The sun and stars as well as the foliate ornament at top and bottom were not original to the roundel. Mid 14th century. Henry Vaughan Bequest. D. 29.2cms (2270-1900)

13
A female saint in an architectural setting under a tall canopy. Probably from Norwich. c.1350. Ht. 1.26m (881-1935)

placed in horizontal bands between areas of 'grisaille' and long thin borders; but in the west window, given in 1338, the canopies have taken the place of the 'grisaille' and fill almost half the area. One of the reasons for the growth of this artistic convention was the architectural change in the shape of windows. The unobstructed spaces of the 12th and 13th centuries gave way to larger, taller apertures with mullions which dictated long thin panels of glass. The opening years of the 14th century saw Early English giving way to Decorated and the emergence of Perpendicular in the 1330s. The tracery lights became very elaborate and glaziers found ingenious ways of filling the complex shapes with shields, donors and angels. In a particularly fine example in St Lucy's chapel in Christchurch Cathedral, Oxford, we find a wide variety of grotesque and diverting creatures closely related to contemporary book illumination.

With the changes in architectural style came a new range of colours. The earlier predominant reds and blues were joined by brown, murrey (mulberry), violet, a dark mossy green and, most important for the future, a new brilliant yellow. This could vary from

14
St John the Evangelist, St James the Less and the Prophet Zephaniah. Painted in the workshop of Thomas of Oxford for the chapel of Winchester College. c.1390. Ht. 3.54m (4237-1855)

a brownish-orange to a pale lemon and was obtained by firing, generally on the outside surface of the glass, a derivative of sulphide of silver. This yellow stain first appeared in the opening decade of the century and soon became extremely popular with glass-painters. It obviated the need to cut a separate piece of yellow glass to provide a halo round a head, for example, and was of great convenience in heraldry and for ornament generally.

The changes in the architectural setting of glass and in the pigments employed were accompanied by a radical development in painting style. The drama and powerful simplification of 12th and 13th century painting was replaced by a more humane, gentle and naturalistic art (plate 12). Many figures have a sweetness, sometimes even a sentimentality, not found earlier and are often shown standing with the weight on one leg, the opposite hip thrust out, so that the body forms an S-shape. Drapery is arranged in a less agitated manner and the background is filled with tight leafy scrolls, which later gave way to continuous lengths of seaweed-like decoration (plate 15). This change of mood is reflected in the use of black pigment, stippling taking the place of smearing, and scratching-out used with greater delicacy. These tendencies can best be seen in the figures of the Virgin and Child and of St Michael at Eaton Bishop, Herefordshire (1317-21) as well as in the St Catherine at Deerhurst, Gloucestershire (c. 1320), who holds the wheel of her martyrdom as if it were a toy. More readily accessible than these is the superb 14th century glass in Wells Cathedral and the enormous quantity in York Minster, where more glass of this period can be seen than anywhere else in England.

By the middle of the century the development of Perpendicular tracery is accompanied by further changes in the style and colour of stained glass. The seven clerestory windows above the choir of Tewkesbury Abbey, Gloucestershire, carried out in about 1340-44 have all the strong subtle colours of the first half of the century. The figures stand four square to the viewer under flat schematic canopies with prominent crockets and vegetal finials on the archictectural niches in which they stand (see plate 13). The general effect is dark and rich in marked contrast to the east window of Gloucester Cathedral, carried out only a few years later in 1347-9. Here the impression given is far paler with red and yellow used with a large quantity of white glass. The painting is more delicate, silver stain is used extensively and the canopies are far taller and more realistic with long thin side shafts serving as borders. Although in its original state the window was appreciably darker, there is none the less a greatly increased and almost austere use of white glass.

More characteristic of late 14th century glass are the windows made by Thomas of Oxford between 1380 and 1404 for the two colleges founded by William of Wykeham in Oxford and Winchester (plate 14). The ante-chapel of New College is thronged with tall grave figures standing in architectural settings of considerable variety and painted with an increasing interest in perspective. The colours used are clearer and lighter and the style shows an awareness of continental painting, notably of the Cologne school. The early 14th century delight in pattern and outline is giving way to a greater pre-occupation with three-dimensional modelling, a tendency which increased during the 15th century.

Besides figures of saints under canopies (plate 15) the most common way of filling windows at this time was with rows of small narrative panels. An impressive example of a window treated in this way is the east window of York Minster made in 1405-08 by John Thornton of Coventry. Both he and Thomas of Oxford must have had workshops of some size to carry out the considerable commissions they were given. Indeed the numbers of glaziers at work had increased enormously in the course of the 14th century, for they are found not only in most towns of any size but also in a surprising number of villages. Indeed by 1364 they were sufficiently numerous to petition to set up their own guild. With the growth in their numbers went an improvement in their position in society and it is significant that Thomas of Oxford felt able to include a portrait of himself kneeling at the foot of the east window he supplied for Winchester College. A post of King's Glazier, which may have existed informally for some time, was now institutionalised when Richard Savage was appointed for life in 1393.

The 15th century saw a further growth in church building and alterations. Windows were made larger still, and an enormous amount of stained glass was painted. Regional styles can now be identified and a York school can be discerned, to take two random examples, in the glass at St Martin's, Coney Street and All Saints, North Street in that city. At East Harling Parish Church and at St Peter Mancroft, Norwich it may be possible to identify the glass of one particular workshop within a more general Norwich school (plate 16). Besides stylistic peculiarities, regional differences can be most readily observed in the painting of the formalised flowers, heraldic badges, birds and so forth which were produced in large numbers on lozenge-shaped quarries as a background to figures or scenes. Such quarries can be seen in many churches and also appear in domestic settings to which they were well suited (plate 17). Hitherto painted glass was unusual in houses but in the 15th century it becomes more common and roundels showing the Signs of the Zodiac or the Labours of the Months are found as well as much heraldry (plate 18). Coats of arms continued to be extensively used in church windows and donor figures became yet more obtrusive. At Long Melford (Suffolk) the clerestory was dominated by almost life size figures of the Clopton family and their connections while at St Neot (Cornwall) whole families are shown kneeling along the bases of the windows.

In two particular respects the 15th century can show a richness not previously found in iconography and in technique. The lives of the saints continued to be popular (plate 19) as did the Life and Passion of

15

16

17

15
St Lawrence holding the grid-iron, the symbol of his martyrdom. Painted by an artist belonging to a Midlands school, who had worked in York. From Hampton Court, Herefordshire. c.1420-35. Ht. 1.12m (C.237-1931)

16
A feathered angel playing a lute. The style and features such as the 'ears of barley' on which the angel stands are characteristic of the Norwich school. c.1460-80. Ht. 61cms (C.338-1937)

17
A panel of quarries painted in yellow silver stain. Besides a bird, animals and flowers there are the crowned 'H' of Henry VII and the 'ER' of Edward VI. 14th to 16th centuries. Henry Vaughan Bequest. Ht. 89.8cms (930-1900)

Christ but we also find the Seven Corporal Works of Mercy, the Seven Sacraments, the Te Deum and the Ten Commandments (plate 20). Old subjects like the Fall of Man and the Joys and Sorrows of the Virgin Mary received a new interpretation. The cumulative effect of a church filled with such didactic windows can be appreciated at Great Malvern Priory which still possesses most of its glass of the first half of the 15th century. In richness of execution, too, the late 15th century is a period of great achievement. Some especially fine examples of the highly sophisticated painting and use of coloured glass which were possible at this time are the windows in the parish church at Tattershall, Lincs (1482), at Browne's Hospital, Stamford (c. 1485) and in the Beauchamp Chapel at St Mary's, Warwick. The Warwick glass was produced by John Prudde, the King's Glazier, between 1447 and 1450. It is known to have been very expensive and to have made use of the finest coloured glass available. Prudde also employed a technique requiring special skill. This was the insertion of 'jewels' into the garments of saints. Holes were drilled into some of the larger pieces of glass and small contrasting pieces were leaded into them, giving the appearance of gems sewn onto rich vestments. The process was a risky one, given the fragility of glass and the primitive nature of the tools then available to the glazier.

The Browne's Hospital glass is still thoroughly medieval in feeling but within ten years work had started on the windows at Fairford, Gloucestershire which clearly belong to the Renaissance. This change in style came from the continent and was largely brought about by foreign artists. Neither of these facts was in itself remarkable. Foreigners had worked in England from the 14th century onwards and continental influences are apparent in English stained-glass from an even earlier period. But in the early 16th century there was an important difference. For the first time Continental glass painters were taken up by the court and Barnard Flower, who came from the Low Countries, became the King's Glazier in about 1505. He had been in England since 1496 and was one of a number of such artists who migrated to England at about this time. Some, like the itinerant band of Flemish glass-painters employed by Lord Sandys at his house, the Vyne, near Basingstoke (Hants) in 1521, did not remain permanently but a number settled in this country, mainly in Southwark. This Southwark school was responsible for or strongly influenced the glass at Hillesden, Bucks (c. 1500) and Withcote, Leicestershire (1537). But their

18
'March' and 'October' from a set of the Labours of the Months, once at Cassiobury Park. First half 15th century. Given by the National Art Collections Fund. D. 20.3cms (C.123 and C.127-1923)

19
A scene from a saint's life, perhaps that of the boy Saint William of Norwich.
Painted in a Norwich workshop.
c.1460-80. Ht. 45.7cms (C.351-1937)

20
Feeding the Hungry from a series of the *Seven Corporal Works of Mercy.* Perhaps from
Coventry. c.1430. D. 16.8cms (C.56-1953)

most important undertaking was undoubtedly the glass in Henry
VII's King's College Chapel at Cambridge. Work began there in 1515
and continued until about 1540. Barnard Flower died in 1517 and was
succeeded both at King's College and as King's Glazier by a Fleming,
Galyon Hone.

At first sight King's College would seem to have been an ideal
commission. A large proportion of the wall area consisted of window
openings and adequate finance was forthcoming. The artists involved
responded superbly to the challenge but the sheer quantity of space to
be filled posed problems. The windows were still divided by the mullions into long narrow strips, a visual proportion in conflict with the
new ideas on the use of pictorial space which were coming in with the
Renaissance. The glass-painters partly overcame this problem by
ignoring the mullions altogether and taking the design right across the
window. This was not in itself an innovation in England: it can be
found in the north transept window at Canterbury showing Edward

IV and his family (c. 1482) as well as in the Magnificat window at Great Malvern Priory (1501). But at King's this device was used with greater ingenuity and conviction, rather as it was on the continent.

The windows of King's College Chapel can be seen to mark the end of the middle ages as far as stained-glass was concerned, and they coincided with a radical change in the fortunes of the glass-painters. For some time in England there had been a puritanical and reformist ground-swell of popular feeling against the enrichment of churches. This movement, as well as Henry VIII's divorce from Catherine of Aragon, led on to the 'Reformation Parliament' of 1529-36 and the Dissolution of the Monasteries of 1536-40. A wave of iconoclasm swept the country and the monasteries as a source of patronage vanished. Any form of religious subject matter was branded as idolatrous with the result that the glass painters lost their most important source of work.

By contrast glaziers had plenty to do replacing pictorial windows. It is not always appreciated that a man described as a glazier in a contemporary document very rarely possessed the necessary skills and equipment to paint on glass. Doubtless many glass-painters were capable of undertaking repair work or plain glazing with white glass but on the whole they depended for their livelihoods on their painting and this aspect of their work was catastrophically curtailed. Fortunately secular work was still available and heraldic painting, in particular, expanded considerably and became the focus of much creative ability (plates 21 & 22). By the end of the 16th century it had become an art form in its own right as can be seen in the remarkable series of panels set in elaborate patterns of clear glazing at Gilling Castle (Yorkshire) carried out by Bernard Dininckhof from 1585.

This development of heraldic painting coincided with a most important technical innovation. Hitherto the only colours which could be painted and fired on to glass were the black used for line-work and yellow silver-stain. In the early 16th century a reddish flesh tint was discovered, which was used in some of the King's College windows and by the middle of the century blue, green and purple were all available. These colours were obtained by grinding up coloured glass, mixing it with a suitable vehicle and firing in a small 'muffle' kiln sealed off from any direct contact with the flame. No longer was it necessary to cut out pieces of pot-metal glass to the often complicated shapes required. Instead the artist had a palette of colours which he could paint onto regular rectangles of clear glass as if he were painting on canvas or panel. Lead-lines became solely utilitarian and were no longer needed to accentuate the painted lines.

During the 16th century these enamel colours were used only sparingly. But the increasing complication of heraldic quarterings made it almost impossible to use pot-metal glass for the various tinctures which had to be cut into minute shapes (plate 22). The problem was easily obviated by painting with enamel-colours and this became the norm. Another of the reasons for the use of enamels was the increasing scarcity of pot-metal glass. During the late 15th century there was a steady decrease in the number of stained glass windows made and this slackening in the demand for pot-metal led to a fall-off in production. As pot-metal became less available there was an increased incentive to use enamels and when political upheavals in France caused the destruction of the Lorraine glass-making industry in 1636, glass painters in England were finally obliged to rely entirely on enamels.

The process of destruction set in train by the Reformation did not affect parish churches immediately. As monastic buildings became redundant they lost their windows through the beating out of the glass for the value of the lead. It was not until Edward VI's Injunctions of 1547, which specifically listed stained-glass amongst church furnishings to be destroyed, that serious damage took place. Even then some parishes preferred to store their glass rather than break it up. It was soon realised that churches were more or less unusable without windows and in the Royal Injunctions of 1559 'preserving nevertheless or repairing the walls and glass' was decreed. Although the tide of destruction receded there were spasmodic outbreaks of inconoclasm and a steady process of new plain glass replacing the old 'superstitious images'.

Towards the end of Elizabeth's reign a movement for liturgical renewal was discernible in the Church of England. At first this was concerned with a return of beauty to the liturgy but it soon came to include the recognition of the importance of the physical setting of worship and the value of images. Once again windows with religious subject matter became acceptable and by 1616 a window showing the Passion had been installed in the chapel of the Trinity Hospital at Greenwich and figures of Christ and apostles at Wadham College, Oxford. Artists such as Robert Rudland, Richard Greenbury, Richard Butler, Lewis Dolphin and Baptista Sutton all received important commissions and can be associated with existing windows. But by far the most significant of the painters practising at this time were two brothers, Bernard and Abraham van Linge, natives of Emden. They came to England in the 1620s and supplied a number of windows, particularly for Oxford colleges. Bernard painted glass for Wadham College (1622) and the Chapel of Lincoln's Inn (c. 1623-26), while Abraham's work can be seen (plate 24) in the Victoria & Albert Museum (from Hampton Court, Herefordshire) and in Oxford at Queen's (1635), Christ Church (c. 1635), Balliol (1637) and University (1641) Colleges. The Hampton Court panel, showing the Deposition, is particularly important not only because it is signed but also as a reflection of current attitudes to the depiction of religious subjects. It is inscribed 'The truth hereof is historicall devine and not superstissious Anno Domini 1629'. There could be no better evidence of the anxiety of the patron to avoid accusations of Popery. Besides religious glass Abraham van Linge was particularly skilled at painting quarries.

21

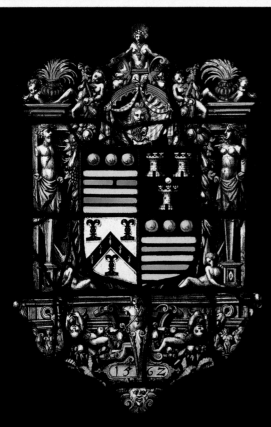

22

23

21
The arms of the Tudors. Said to have come from
Cowick Priory, Devon. Mid 16th century. Ht. 40.1cms
(452-1919)

22
The arms of Pigott quartering Castelline and Walcott
in a classical setting characteristic of the northern
Renaissance. Dated 1562. Given by W Coker Iliffe. Ht.
61cms (C.126-1929)

23
The arms of Beaupré and Fodringaye from Beaupré
Hall, Cambridgeshire. c.1570. Given by Mrs L S
Kinsman. Ht. 76.5cms (C.63-1945)

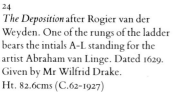

24
The Deposition after Rogier van der
Weyden. One of the rungs of the ladder
bears the intials A-L standing for the
artist Abraham van Linge. Dated 1629.
Given by Mr Wilfrid Drake.
Ht. 82.6cms (C.62-1927)

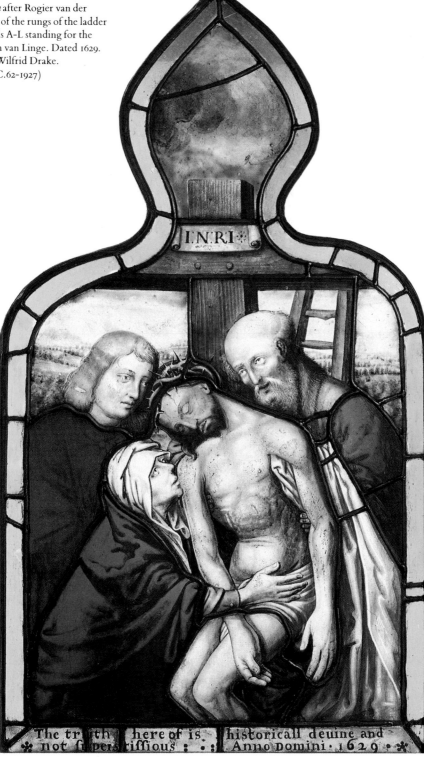

24

27

25
The arms and cypher of Charles II. Perhaps from the George Inn, Coney Street,
York. c.1680-85. Given by Mrs George Milner. Ht. 88.9cms
(C.88-1926)

There are some charming examples at Lydiard Tregoze, Wilts (c. 1629)
with flowers, animals, birds, fruits and figures, all taken from print
sources. The best known window of this type, now in the Victoria &
Albert Museum, came from Betley Hall, Staffs. It celebrates 'A Mery
May' and has a maypole, a Maid of the May, a hobby-horse and Morris
dancers (cover illustration).

Although the so-called Laudian revival had a considerable effect on
church decoration, it was only for a comparatively short period. The
Civil War broke out in 1642 and with it renewed iconoclasm. Many
documents survive giving a good idea of how attitudes differed. On
the one hand the diary of William Dowsing, Parliamentary Visitor to
East Anglia, describes the systematic and zealous manner in which he
oversaw the smashing of everything he considered idolatrous. On the
other hand some parishes, like Toft Monks in Norfolk, took down the
glass with care and reinstated it later. Few churches were spared and
even cathedrals like Winchester did not escape. The vast area of
jumbled fragments in its west window bears tragic witness to puritan
violence.

It was not until the end of the Commonwealth and the restoration
of Charles II in 1660 that glass-painting flourished once again.
Abraham van Linge appears to have ceased working when the Civil
War began and the man who emerged as the most successful artist of
the late 17th century was Henry Gyles of York (1645-1709). There is no
evidence as to where he learnt his craft and he may have been largely

self-taught. Although he painted a few figurative panels his main speciality was heraldic work, in which he excelled, as can be seen at Acomb (York, 1663), Staveley (Derby, 1676), Adel (Yorks, 1681) and in a panel (plate 25) from York c. 1680-85 now in the Victoria & Albert Museum. He also painted glass sundials of which a number survive. A particularly ambitious example at Tong Hall near Bradford has a sun in the centre and figures of the Seasons at the four corners.

By the end of the 17th century glass-painting in England was at an extremely low ebb. It is symptomatic that there appears to have been no one in York from whom Henry Gyles could have learned. That the situation in London was no better we know from a letter to Gyles from his friend Francis Place written in July 1683. Place had discovered from William Price, a glass-painter, that 'there is 4 in Towne but not worke enough to Imploy one' and he observes of Price that 'I perceave his cheife traid is glasing by wc. I belejve he gets a greate deele of Mony for he is belejved Rich'. Price was born in the mid-17th century and was Master of the Glaziers' Company in 1699. Although he painted a Nativity for Christ Church, Oxford and a window with scenes from the life of Christ for Merton College (still surviving in storage) his work seems to have been mainly heraldic. His son Joshua (1672-1722) went into partnership with him and was responsible for the east window of Queen's College, Oxford (1717), ten panels for Lord Chandos (1719-21) and the rose window in the north transept of West-minster Abbey (1721-23). The commission from Lord Chandos was for the chapel of Cannons, his great house in Middlesex. When it was pulled down in 1747 Joshua Price's son William, also a glass-painter, was employed by Lord Foley to install the panels in the chapel at Great Whitley (Worcestershire) where they can still be seen.

The three members of the Price family dominate English glass-painting in the first half of the 18th century. The younger, William Price (c. 1703-65), was a master of the rococo idiom and his consider-able output included the east window of St Martin-in-the-Fields (1726), the west window of Westminster Abbey (1735), the windows on the south side of the chancel of New College, Oxford (c. 1735-40) as well as settings for older glass in the parish church of Preston-on-Stour, Warwickshire (1754) and for Horace Walpole at Strawberry Hill (1754 and 1759). His windows at New College incorporate medieval glass and both there and at Preston-on-Stour he shows a well-developed antiquarian interest.

The collections of old stained glass formed by Horace Walpole and a number of his contemporaries interested in medieval art and archi-tecture gave impetus to the early stirrings of the Gothic Revival, which was to be of such importance for the resurgence of stained glass in the 19th century. Besides being a patron of William Price, Walpole played a part in the careers of the three most important glass-painters of the second half of the 18th century. When Price retired he turned to William Peckitt of York (1731-95) to carry on minor work on Straw-berry Hill; like Gyles before him, Peckitt seems to have been self-

26

27

30

28

26
A lunette from the upper part of a
window in the porch of Harleyford
Manor, Buckinghamshire. Painted by
William Collins. c.1820. Given by
Harleyford Estate Ltd. Ht. 47.5cms
(C.72 to b-1980)

27
The Last Supper. Painted in enamel
colours by William Peckitt and set
within a simulated gilt frame. c.1780.
Given by Mr J A Knowles. Ht. 61cms
(C.180-1934)

28
St George and the Dragon. Inscribed
'Designed and executed by C.E. Gwilt,
1840'. Ht. 88.3cms (C.315-1976)

taught. Almost all his work was in the north of England but, like Price, he worked at New College, Oxford (1765 and 1772-4) and he also supplied the west window of Exeter Cathedral in 1766 using cartoons which had once belonged to Price. Although little of the Exeter window survives, much of his New College glass is still extant as are his Last Supper at Audley End, Cambs (1771) and a library window at Trinity College, Cambridge (1775). Peckitt was not skilled at figure painting and relied on cartoons by other artists notably Biagio Rebecca and Giovanni Battista Cipriani. The cartoons he had used at Exeter had probably been provided for William Price by Sir James Thornhill who had also supplied Joshua Price. None of these artists made any concession in their designs to glass as a medium and it is clear that Peckitt and his contemporaries thought largely, if not entirely, in terms of trying to produce transparent oil-paintings. In two of his works, a self portrait in the York Art Gallery and a Last Supper in the Victoria & Albert Museum (plate 27), Peckitt even went so far as to include a simulated gilt picture frame.

The best-known surviving example of this pictorial approach is the Nativity in the west window of New College, Oxford. This was painted by Thomas Jervais (died 1799) after a design by Sir Joshua Reynolds and aroused strong feelings, both for and against, when it was installed in 1783. Jervais was an Irishman who came to England in 1770 with an introduction to Walpole from Lord Charlemont. It is not known whether Walpole furthered his career in any way, but it is possible that he did for we know that his compatriot James Pearson (c. 1739-1838) seems to have been indebted to Walpole for his first important commission. This was the east window of Ely Cathedral, only a small part of which survives. Pearson went on to do the east window of the clerestory of Salisbury Cathedral (1781) and glass for Beckford at Fonthill (1798). Both Pearson and Jervais specialised in small decorative panels, often after old masters, intended for domestic settings (plate 29). A fashion developed for installing painted glass in the upper part of a window with plain glazing below so as not to obstruct the view. Windows of this kind are found at Strawberry Hill and the same idea was followed at Eaton Hall, near Chester and Harleyford Manor, near Marlow.

Both these houses contained glass by William Collins who had premises in the Strand. Plate 26 shows a characteristic example of his work. The oval scene with its surround of flowers is painted with great delicacy but the vivid border round it is typical of the bright colours and greater vulgarity of much Regency glass. The early 19th century saw the increased use of painted glass in public buildings and Royal palaces, such as the Pavilion at Brighton. Apart from Collins other prominent artists working in the pictorial tradition at this time were Joseph Backler and William Raphael Eginton (1778-1834). Most of their work was in a classical manner but Eginton produced a number of windows, notably at Brockley near Bristol, which show an interest

29
A ruin beside a river. Signed and dated
'James Pearson, London, 1789'.
Ht. 49.8cms (C.134-1977)

in medieval glass painting and a wish to emulate the style of the 14th
century.

Antiquarian interest in the middle ages was growing and with it a
knowledge of medieval technical skills (plate 28). This process was
accelerated by the information gained from extensive restorations of
early glass carried out at this time. Betton and Evans of Shrewsbury,
for example, made painstaking copies of the 14th century windows at
Winchester College in 1821-28 and worked on the glass of St
Lawrence's, Ludlow in 1832. Although the results may seem crude
today they were a considerable advance on anything done before and
show that the firm had learnt much from their commissions.

The most important designer of the early 19th century to be
concerned with historical styles of glass-painting was undoubtedly
Thomas Willement (1786-1871). Although grounded in the pictorial
manner of the 18th century he shows in his work an awareness of the
flat backgrounds and limited three-dimensional nature of medieval
stained-glass (plate 30). It is clear that he realised the value of leading

30

34

30
The Presentation. Designed by Thomas Willement for Holy Trinity, Carlisle. 1845.
Given by the Diocese of Carlisle. Ht. 1.43m (C.150-1980)

31
The Advent of Beatrice from Dante's *Purgatoria*. Designed by N H J Westlake and
executed by Lavers and Barraud. 1864. Ht. 1.44m (780-1864)

32
A welcoming angel designed by C E Kempe and executed by his firm for *Old Place*,
his own house at Lindfield. c.1890. Ht. 82cms (C.64-1978)

not only as a means of holding together pieces of different coloured glass but also as a way of emphasising the design. Although these fundamental qualities are apparent in his work as early as 1829 (Butleigh, Somerset), his comparative ignorance of historical styles and the limited range of coloured glass available to him inevitably detracted from his attempts to produce an authentic effect. Both these disadvantages were largely overcome during the 1840s when four books appeared which established the basic sequence and development of style in English medieval glass-painting. They were James Ballantine's *A Treatise on Painted Glass* (1845), Charles Winston's *An Inquiry into the Difference of Style Observable in Ancient Glass Painting, Especially in England,* and *Hints on Glass Painting* (2 Vols 1847) and William Warrington's *History of Stained Glass* (1848). In 1849 Charles Winston had chemical analyses made of samples of medieval glass and he persuaded James Powell of the Whitefriars Glass Works to produce glass to the formulae he discovered. This new 'antique' glass gave a far wider and more subtle range of colours than had hitherto been available and Powell's lead was followed a few years later by another range made by the firm of W E Chance of Birmingham.

Thomas Willement had a lasting influence on the Gothic Revival, not only through his works but also through his pupils. Two who became major manufacturers in the first half of the 19th century were William Warrington (1786-1869) and Michael O'Connor (1801-67), both of whom have a particular importance since they served as a link with A W N Pugin. Of all the gothicists of the period Pugin was the most committed, energetic and productive. Besides Warrington and O'Connor, Pugin used William Wailes (1808-81) and, above all, John Hardman, to make his windows. His sensitive but powerful and well-informed designs, as well as his proselytising zeal, made Pugin a formidable propagandist. With the support of the Anglo-Catholic revival and the influential work of the Cambridge Camden Society, Gothic had emerged by the middle of the 19th century as the dominant style in English stained glass.

Besides witnessing the triumph of Gothicism over pictorialism the period of 1840-1860 also saw an enormous growth in the demand for stained-glass. Increasing numbers of churches were being built and in about 1840 the fashion emerged for stained-glass windows to be given as memorials. This created an insatiable demand which only began to taper off after 1870. Many new stained-glass companies came into existence throughout the country, but although the majority were small firms, at least three quarters of the work went to the largest manufacturers almost all of which were based in London. Architects often had favourite designers whose work suited their buildings and William Butterfield's preference for Alexander Gibbs (1832-86) and G E Street's for Wailes and Hardman, for example, tended to place the available work in fewer hands. The most prolific studio from its start in

1855 right up to the First World War seems to have been Clayton and Bell. Besides those firms already mentioned, Heaton Butler and Bayne, Lavers and Barraud (plate 31), C E Kempe (plate 32), Burlison and Grylls, Joseph Bell of Bristol and Shrigley and Hunt of Lancaster all enjoyed considerable success in the second half of the 19th century, producing windows in the wide variety of styles demanded by changing fashion.

The foundation by William Morris and his friends of Morris, Marshall, Faulkner and Co in 1861 coincided with the end of the first and most fervent phase of the Gothic Revival. Although the earliest windows of Edward Burne-Jones, Morris's principal designer, are in a strongly medieval idiom (plate 33) he soon showed himself to be happiest when working in a very personal and more classical manner. Walter Pater's book on the Renaissance written between 1868 and 1873 encouraged a classical revival and slowly fashion veered away from narrow medievalism towards a freer interpretation of Gothic forms. Artists no longer felt obliged to vie with each other in producing a yet more 'correct' version of some earlier style, but took what they wanted from the past in a new spirit of eclecticism. The slavish imitation of medieval mannerisms steadily diminished but conventions such as canopies, albeit in barely recognisable form, survive to this day. The academic and more narrow approach of the first half of the 19th century was roundly condemned by Henry Holiday (1839-1927), in particular, who became the chief designer for James Powell & Sons of Whitefriars in London and emerged as a major figure in the classical revival. The windows of his maturity have great movement with statuesque figures against sumptuous backgrounds of rich foliage which owe a considerable debt to Morris.

The Aesthetic movement of the 1870s could not have taken place without the classical revival or the work of Burne-Jones (plate 34) and Holiday. Avant-garde artists started using softer and paler colours and discarded the diamond-shaped quarry characteristic of medieval glass, prefering rectangles, sometimes painted with sun-flowers or semi-oriental motifs associated with the new interest in Japanese art. Shrigley and Hunt of Lancaster became particular exponents of the new wave but few designers and manufacturers remained untouched by what a contemporary critic termed 'a strong tendency towards greenish-jaundice'.

In 1882 the Century Guild of Artists was formed, followed by the foundation of the Art Workers Guild in 1884 and the Arts and Crafts Exhibition Society in 1888. This flurry of activity amongst architects, artists and designers reflected a disenchantment with mass-production. The artist rarely had any contact with his design once it was in the hands of the manufacturer and was frequently deeply disappointed with the result when he eventually saw it. Those founders of the Arts and Crafts Movement who were concerned with stained-

33
St Peter sinking in the Sea of Tiberias.
Designed by Edward Burne-Jones and
executed by James Powell and Sons.
1857. Ht. 1.73m (C.62-1976)

34
*How Galahad sought the sangreal and
found it because his heart was single so he
followed it to Sarras the city of the spirit.*
Designed by Sir Edward Burne-Jones
for his own house, 'The Grange', in
Fulham. Painted by Dearle in the studio
of William Morris and Co in 1886.
Given by Sir Philip Burne-Jones.
Ht. 45.7cms (C.625-1920)

35
The Brownies, fairies who carry out
household tasks at night while humans
are asleep. Designed by Selwyn Image
probably for Soham House, New-
market. c.1895. Ht. 80cms. (C.118 to
c.1984)

glass, notably Selwyn Image (1849-1930) (plate 35) and Christopher Whall (1849-1924), were determined to make their own windows themselves or to supervise the manufacturing process closely. Their view was shared by Mary Lowndes (1857-1929), and Alfred Drury (1868-1940) who started a company in 1897 bearing their joint names. Its purpose was to provide studios for artists and workshops with qualified craftsmen in the same building. Their first premises were in Chelsea but they soon moved to the Glass House in Fulham, a specially designed building, which still exists as a continuing memorial to the ideals of the Arts and Crafts Movement.

Coinciding with this movement was the production of a new range of glass, known as Prior's Early English or Slab glass. This was made by the Southwark firm of Britten and Gilson at the suggestion of the architect E S Prior. It varied considerably in thickness and had strong streaks and variations in colour, adding significantly to the artist's freedom of choice. The greater possibilities offered by the new glass and the facilities of Lowndes and Drury led to a great release of individuality which was to have the most profound effect on the future development of stained-glass in England.

Of all the Arts and Crafts stained-glass artists the most influential in terms of his followers was Christopher Whall (plate 36). In 1898 he began teaching at the Royal College and a year later he became a lecturer at the Central School of Arts and Crafts. Reginald Hallward, Louis Davis, Hugh Arnold and Karl Parsons were amongst his better-known pupils and his influence extended yet further. He was asked to teach at the Dublin Metropolitan School of Art and arranged for A E Child, one of his leading pupils, to go instead. Child helped to establish the 'Tower of Glass' studios which were crucial for the development of stained-glass in Ireland and which fostered the careers of Henry Clarke, Wilhelmina Geddes and Evie Hone. In a similar manner Whall's pupil Henry Payne took up a teaching post at Birmingham thus influencing the Bromsgrove Guild through his pupil A J Davis.

Another significant figure in the Arts and Crafts Movement was Robert Anning Bell (1863-1933) who was also to teach at the Royal College of Art. He had previously been a lecturer in Glasgow where an important group of artists were making stained-glass in the latter part of the 19th century. The best known of these was Charles Rennie Mackintosh (1868-1928) but Daniel Cottier, Stephen Adam, J & W Guthrie and, somewhat later, Douglas Strachan were all producing windows of high quality and strong individuality.

36
St Chad and *St Agatha*. These figures are smaller replicas of lights made in 1900 for Gloucester Cathedral Lady Chapel. Designed by C W Whall and made by his studio. c.1910. Given by Mr C J Whall. Ht. 78cms (C.87&88-1978)

37
A standing female figure designed and
made by Leonard Walker as a war
memorial in St Lawrence, Brondesbury.
c.1918. Given by the Church Commis-
sioners. Ht. 46cms (C.2-1973)

38
The Virgin and Child. Designed and
painted by Evie Hone. c.1953.
Given by Mr John E Lowe. Ht. 46.5cms
(C.118-1965)

39
A landscape designed by Roger Fry
after a picture by Cézanne. Made in the
Omega Workshops for General Sir Ian
Hamilton's house in Hyde Park
Gardens. 1913. Given by Mr Donald
Hamilton. Ht. 1.29m (C.80-1950)

In the early years of the 20th century the division grew wider between the large companies with their own studio designers and individual artists, often working on their own (plate 37). On the whole the companies were more conservative, continuing along traditional lines, although Whitefriars Studio, for example, encouraged a certain degree of experiment under James Hogan. Such freedom for the individual within the context of a large firm was unusual in this century and certainly was not the case in C E Kempe's old company. Although the firm's windows had no lasting influence, he himself was of considerable importance as the master of J Ninian Comper (1864-1960), who evolved an academic style based on medieval glass, the effects of which can still be discerned today. The essence of this style depended on good draughtsmanship of a highly representational kind, light colours including much yellow stain and the extensive use of white glass. It is a tradition running through the work of Comper's pupil Martin Travers, the brothers G F and C R Webb and Hugh Easton.

In marked contrast there are the artists who followed a non-representational path, using strong colours, experimental technique and a more expressionist attitude. Apart from these qualities their work had nothing in common other than an awareness of modern painting on the continent. French post-impressionism was the dominant influences on the Omega Workshops and the Victoria & Albert Museum is fortunate in possessing their only surviving window. This is a near-abstract roundel of great size designed by Roger Fry in 1914 after a landscape by Cézanne (plate 39). Another entirely abstract example of this period is the west window of St Mary's, Slough, by Alfred Wolmark installed in 1915.

No further glass in such a modern style was to be commissioned until after the Second World War when Evie Hone (plate 38) was asked to design the east window of Eton College Chapel (1949-52) and Erwin Bossanyi made two windows for Canterbury Cathedral (1956). Although much stained-glass was produced in England, particularly in the immediate post-war period of war damage repair work, very few new churches were being built where glass of more modern design would have been appropriate. It was not until the construction of Coventry Cathedral in the mid 1950s that an important commission was given to a group of artists fully committed to the modern movement. Lawrence Lee, Geoffrey Clarke and Keith New provided the windows for the nave, Margaret Traherne made those for the Chapel of Unity and John Piper designed the vast window for the Baptistry, which was made by Patrick Reyntiens (plate 40). This commission was of the greatest importance in the history of 20th-century English stained glass but it did not immediately lead to an increased demand for modern windows.

More recently however a new public awareness of the decorative possibilities of stained glass in secular as well as in ecclesiastical settings has increased demand and widened the opportunities for artists. An important exhibition of English glass held at Chartres in 1982 showed that they have responded to this stimulus and that the English tradition remains as vigorous and varied as ever (plate 41).

40
Christ between St Peter and St Paul. The
composition is based on a Romanesque
tympanum at Aulnay in France.

Designed by John Piper and made by
Patrick Reyntiens. c.1958. Ht. 82.5cms
(C.77-1981)

41
On a Theme of the sea. Designed and
made by Caroline Swash. 1979.
Ht. 1.02m (C.29-1980)

Further Reading

General Bibliographies
M H Caviness, *Stained Glass before 1540*, Boston, 1983
D Evans, *A Bibliography of Stained Glass*, Bury St Edmunds, 1982

Periodicals
Both the above bibliographies list the contents of the *Journal of the British Society of Master Glass-Painters*. This is the only journal produced in England relating to stained glass. The Stained Glass Association of America produces a quarterly entitled *Stained Glass* which also contains material relating to English stained glass.

General
J Baker, *English Stained Glass*, London (1960)
B Clarke (editor), *Architectural Stained Glass*, London (1979)
B Coe, *Stained Glass in England: 1150-1550*, London (1981)
Lewis F Day, *Windows*, London (1879)
M Drake, *A History of English Glass Painting*, London (1912)
F S Eden, *Ancient Stained Glass*, Cambridge (1913)
E S Godfrey, *The Development of English Glassmaking 1560-1640*, Oxford (1975)
M Harrison, *Victorian Stained Glass*, London (1980)
L Lee, *Stained Glass*, Oxford (1969)
L Lee, *The Appreciation of Stained Glass*, Oxford (1977)
E Liddall Armitage, *Stained Glass*, London (1959)
P Nelson, *Ancient Painted Glass in England 1170-1500*, London (1913)
J Piper, *Stained Glass: Art or Anti-Art*, London (1968)
Bernard Rackham, *A Guide to the Collection of Stained Glass, Victoria & Albert Museum*, London (1936)
H Read, *English Stained Glass*, London & New York (1926)
R Sowers, *Stained Glass, An Architectural Art*, New York (1965)
N H J Westlake, *A History in the Design of Painted Glass*, London & Oxford, 4 Vols., (1881-94)
C Winston, *An Inquiry into the Differences of Style Observable in Ancient Glass Paintings especially in England; with Hints on Glass Painting*, Oxford & London (1862)
C Winston, *Memoirs illustrative of the art of Glass Painting*, London (1865)
C Woodforde, *English Stained and Painted Glass*, Oxford (1954)

Particular
M H Caviness, *The Windows of Christ Church Cathedral Canterbury*, London (1981)
L S Colchester, *Stained Glass in Wells Cathedral*, Wells (1973)
F M Drake, 'The Painted Glass of Exeter Cathedral and other Devon Churches', *The Archaeological Journal*, Vol LXX (1913)
E W Ganderton and J Lafond, *Ludlow Stained and Painted Glass*, Ludlow (1961)
M A Green, 'Old Painted Glass in Worcestershire', *Worcestershire Archaeological Society*, New Series, Vols. xi-xxix

F Harrison, *The Painted Glass of York*, London (1927)
J Haselock & D O'Connor 'The Medieval Stained Glass of Durham Cathedral', *Medieval Art and Architecture at Durham Cathedral*, London (1980), pp. 105-129
J A Knowles, *Essays in the History of The York School of Glass-Painting*, London (1936)
J D Le Couteur, *Ancient Glass in Winchester*, Winchester (1920)
M Lewis, *Stained Glass in North Wales up to 1850*, Altrincham (1970)
R Marks, 'The Medieval Stained Glass of Wells Cathedral' in L S Colchester (editor), *Wells Cathedral, A History*, Shepton Mallet (1982)
P Moore, *The Stained Glass of Ely Cathedral*, Ely (1973)
N J Morgan, *The Medieval Painted Glass of Lincoln Cathedral*, London (1983)
P A Newton, *The County of Oxford*, London (1979)
E O'Connor and J Haselock, 'The Stained and Painted Glass', Chapter VIII in G E Aylmer and R Cant (editors), *A History of York Minster*, Oxford (1977)
A V Peatling, 'Ancient Stained and Painted Glass in the Churches of Surrey', *Surrey Archaeological Society* (1930)
S A Pitcher, 'Ancient Stained Glass in Gloucestershire Churches', *Transactions Bristol and Gloucestershire Archaeological Society Vol. XLVII*
B Rackham, *The Ancient Glass of Canterbury Cathedral*, London (1949)
M H Ridgway, 'An Introduction to the Making of Coloured Window Glass with special reference to the early Glass Destroyed and Extant in Cheshire', *Chester Archaeological Society Journal*, Vol XXXVII, Part I (1948)
G McN Rushforth, *Medieval Christian Imagery as Illustrated by the Painted Windows of Great Malvern Priory Church*, Oxford (1936)
A C Sewter, *The Stained Glass of William Morris and his Circle*, Yale (1974 & 1975)
R O C Spring, *The Stained Glass of Salisbury Cathedral*, Salisbury (1973)
H Wayment, *The Windows of King's College Chapel Cambridge*, London (1972)
C Woodforde, *Guide to the Medieval Glass in Lincoln Cathedral*, London (1933)
C Woodforde, *Stained Glass in Somerset, 1250-1830*, London (1946)
C Woodforde, *The Norwich School of Glass Painting in the 15th Century*, London (1950)
C Woodforde, *The Stained Glass of New College, Oxford*, Oxford (1951)

Technical
P Reyntiens, *The Technique of Stained Glass*, London (1977)
C W Whall, *Stained Glass Work*, London (1905)

Der Gläſer.

Seufftz nach dem Licht, das nie gebricht.

Das Licht nicht aus dem Haus zutreiben,
bedient man sich der reinen Scheiben;
Jedoch des Hertzens schönes Hauß
will mannig immer dunckler machen,
durch Holtz und Stein der eitlen Sache,
und schließt des Himmels Licht hinaus.